BODY IMAGE

how to love yourself, live life to the fullest,
and celebrate all kinds of bodies

by **Mel Hammond**
illustrated by **Maike Plenzke**

Published by American Girl Publishing

No part of this book may be used or reproduced in any manner whatsoever without written permission except in the case of brief quotations embodied in critical articles and reviews.

22 23 24 25 26 27 QP 10 9 8 7 6 5 4 3 2 1

Editorial Development: Melissa Hammond, Barbara Stretchberry
Art Direction and Design: Jessica Rogers
Illustrations: Maike Plenzke
Production: Jessica Bernard, Caryl Boyer, Jodi Knueppel, Cynthia Stiles
Special thanks: Alys Brooks, Valorie Schaefer

The Consultants

Rebekah Taussig, PhD, earned her doctorate in creative nonfiction and disability studies and writes essays about her life as a disabled person who uses a wheelchair.

Carly Guss, MD, MPH, is a physician at Boston Children's Hospital. She specializes in adolescent medicine, eating disorders, and gender-affirming medical care for youth and young adults.

All Things Bright and Beautiful on page 67 used by permission of the artist and Hauser & Wirth. © Amy Sherald

Self-Portrait with the Portrait of Doctor Farill on page 67 © 2021 Banco de México Diego Rivera Frida Kahlo Museums Trust, Mexico, D.F. / Artists Rights Society (ARS), New York

Library of Congress Cataloging-in-Publication Data
Names: Hammond, Mel, author. | Plenzke, Maike, illustrator.
Title: Smart girl's guide : body image : how to love yourself, live life to
   the fullest, and celebrate all kinds of bodies / by Mel Hammond ;
   illustrated by Maike Plenzke.
Other titles: Body image
Description: 1 Edition. | Middleton : American Girl, 2022. | Series: A
   smart girl's guide | Audience: Ages 10+
Identifiers: LCCN 2021006233 | ISBN 9781683371908 (paperback)
Subjects: LCSH: Self-esteem in adolescence. | Body image in adolescence. |
   Young women—Attitudes
Classification: LCC BF724.3.S36 H37 2022 | DDC 155.5/182—dc23
LC record available at https://lccn.loc.gov/2021006233

americangirl.com/service

Not all services are available in all countries.

Dear Reader,

No matter who you are or where you live, you have a body. And it's amazing! You can use your body to explore the world, meet interesting people, dream, and so much more. How cool is that?

When you were very young, you probably didn't think much about how your body looked. But now that you're getting older, you might find yourself looking in the mirror more often or comparing yourself to other kids. You might also be worried about how your body is changing as you go through puberty. Suddenly, your body might seem like the most important thing in the world.

This book is a feel-good reminder that all bodies are good bodies. In these pages, you'll see all kinds of bodies: big bodies and small bodies, bodies with disabilities, bodies of different races and ethnicities, and bodies with different gender identities and expressions. That's because each and every body is unique and deserves respect. Yes, including yours!

Read on to find activities, tips, crafts, real-girl stories, and everything you need to know about developing a healthy body image. Remember, you and your body are on the same team! No matter how your body looks now or how it changes in the future, you deserve to feel comfortable and proud of who you are.

Your friends at American Girl

contents

BODY IMAGE BASICS

Body image is the way you think and feel about your body.

Having a positive body image helps you do the things you love without worrying about what your body looks like while you do them. You can use your body to express the true you, fully and completely.

No matter what size or shape your body is, what it looks like, or how it changes in the future, you can enjoy all the amazing things your body can do. Starting . . . now!

7

the body blues

Everyone worries about their body sometimes, even the most confident girls you know. And it's no wonder—messages about how girls' bodies "should" look appear all over the place:

Magazines and books

Social media

TV and movies

Advertisements

Mannequins at clothing stores

If you've got the body blues, you're not alone. In fact, over half of girls in third, fourth, and fifth grades say they're unhappy with their bodies. But no one body size, shape, color, ability, or gender is better than any other. *All* bodies are good.

The great news is that there are steps you can take to ward off that worry and embrace your unique self.

Quiz

body image check-up

Is your body image cheering you on or holding you back?

1. Your friend invites you to a pool party to celebrate the first day of summer. Your first thought is . . .

   a. Fun! I can practice my cannonball.

   b. Uh-oh. How will I look in my swimsuit?

   c. No way am I putting on a swimsuit. I'll just pretend I'm sick.

2. What do you love most about your body?

   a. I love all the amazing things I can do in this body!

   b. I like the way certain parts of my face, hair, and body look.

   c. Honestly, nothing about my body is that great.

NEW STUDENT
SONIA

3. During math class, your teacher introduces Sonia, a new student. She has the smoothest skin you've ever seen! What thought crosses your mind?

   a. I hope she's nice. Maybe we can be friends!

   b. Does my skin look like hers? Maybe I need a new skin-care routine.

   c. My skin looks horrible compared to hers. Everyone will like her more than they like me.

4. How much time do you spend in front of the mirror every day?

   a. Long enough to brush my teeth and do my hair.

   b. Less than an hour. Sometimes I like what I see, and other times I don't.

   c. Sometimes I stare at my face and body for hours, thinking about all the things I wish I could change.

5. You're about to audition for a big role in a play, but an older girl says you don't look right for the part. You . . .

   a. laugh it off. You know you look great, and you've been practicing all week!

   b. write on your audition form that you're only interested in a background role.

   c. skip tryouts. Auditioning would just make you feel worse about yourself.

6. You spot a shooting star in the night sky. What do you wish for?

a. A spot on the basketball team. Wait, no! A trip to Paris. Or maybe that I grow up to be president! I can't choose.

b. A few improvements to the way I look

c. A whole new body

7. You're looking through photos from your class trip to the Grand Canyon. What's on your mind?

a. I had so much fun! It felt so good to be outside.

b. How do I look? Maybe I should've worn something different that day.

c. These pictures are terrible. I wish I'd stayed home.

Answers

Mostly a's: You're a **buddy to your body.** You appreciate the life your body allows you to live, and you're pretty happy with the way you look. You listen to your body and try to give it the food, movement, and rest it needs to feel good. You might worry about your appearance every now and then, and that's OK. Keep practicing body love, and you'll be able to hold your head high as your body continues to grow and change!

Mostly b's: You're riding a **body image seesaw.** You like the way you look . . . sometimes. Other times, you focus on the things you'd like to change. You wish you didn't think so much about your body, but you can't help it. With a little boost of body love, you'll be on your way to a happier partnership with your body.

Mostly c's: You're **body stressed and obsessed.** It seems like life would be easier if you could switch bodies with someone else. There's a lot you'd love to do in life, but it all feels impossible with the way your body looks and feels. You're not alone, and it's not your fault you feel this way. Reading this book is a great first step toward loving yourself and living life to the fullest!

loving your body right now

No matter what your body looks or feels like, and no matter how it changes in the future, you can start loving it—right now.

Loving your body means respecting and accepting it no matter . . .

how much it weighs.

what it looks like.

what shape it is.

how different it looks from other bodies.

how it moves.

what special care, medicine, or adaptive equipment it needs.

how it changes in the future.

Awesome affirmations

Throughout this book, look for Body Image Boost activities to help develop a healthy body image. Here's one to get you started.

Grab some colorful sticky notes and write something awesome about yourself on each one. This is called an *affirmation.* Aim for affirmations that celebrate who you are, not what your body looks like.

I'm a good friend.

I'M smart.

My friends can count on me.

I tell hilarious jokes.

There's no one else like me.

I give great hugs.

I'M confident.

Stick these notes to your bathroom mirror, in your locker, inside your planner, above your bed, or anywhere else you can see them. Every day, read your affirmations out loud to remind yourself how awesome you are.

body bliss

What's so great about developing a positive body image? It's important for your health!

Loving your body can lead to:

Confidence

Strong mental health

Happiness

Healthy eating and exercise habits

High self-esteem (liking who you are, inside and out)

Determination to achieve your goals

Long story short: loving your body is good for you!

17

shape and size

A lot of girls worry that their bodies are too big, too small, or the "wrong" shape. But the truth is, bodies of all sizes can be healthy. Doctors use many measurements—including weight—to help make sure you're growing at a healthy rate. For example, losing weight during a growth spurt could mean that something is off. But on its own, a number on a scale doesn't tell you much of anything about your health.

Many people think they can control their body's shape or weight by eating certain foods and exercising. Eating nutritious food and moving your body are great for your health—but they won't necessarily change how your body looks. For the most part, your body shape comes from your *genes,* the code you inherit from your biological parents. So if the women in your family have wide hips and rounded bellies, there's a good chance you'll grow into a similar shape.

In one study, scientists studied people who were adopted as babies. Even though the children ate and exercised in the same ways as their adoptive families, they grew up to have bodies much more similar to their biological parents. In other words, your genes play a bigger role in body size than the way you eat and exercise!

Help!

Whenever I look in the mirror, I think I have too much fat. Nothing I try is helping me with weight loss, but I want to do something fast! Can you tell me the quickest and best way to lose weight?

Ava, California

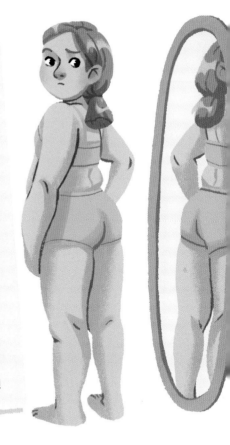

Part of growing up means adding fat to your body, especially on your hips, butt, and breasts. Fat keeps your body warm, gives it energy, protects your organs, and helps protect you against illness. While you're growing, your body needs fat to reach its full potential. Right now, it's natural for your body to gain weight, not lose it!

I'm 10 years old and I'm REALLY worried about my weight because I weigh more than my friends. I look fine when I wear clothes, but when I look in a mirror, I feel uncomfortable about my body. My doctor said that my weight is fine, but I'm not sure if I should start a diet or exercise more. I want to be like my friends, but I bet it's going to take a long time to lose that many pounds. Can you help me?

Harper, Maryland

All girls grow at different rates, and you can't force your body to be the same size as someone else's. Imagine taking care of two trees—one large and one small. Would you stop watering the large tree to stunt its growth, so it looks more like the small tree? No! Both trees deserve plenty of water so they can reach their full potential.

You're you! There's no use trying to be like anyone else. Trust your doctor when she says your weight is healthy. Focus on what you love about *your* body. Feed your body well, move it every day, and help it grow into the best body it can be.

This summer I've been worrying too much about my appearance (mostly my belly), because all my friends and family are super skinny. I love swimming, and everyone wears bikinis, but I think I look terrible in them. PLEASE HELP!

Zoe, Michigan

You have the right to have fun swimming no matter what your body looks like. If you don't feel comfortable wearing a bikini, try a different kind of swimsuit. But if you love bikinis, wear them! Try on a variety of styles and colors until you find one that makes you feel awesome. And if someone at the pool looks at your bikini in a way you don't like, say, "My body is my business, and I like the way it looks." Or just ignore the person!

the skin you're in

From the top of your head to the tips of your toes, your skin's got you covered. Skin does important jobs like protecting your insides, keeping your body the right temperature, and warning you to get away from things that are painful.

Skin can also play a big role in how you feel about your body. Markings like freckles, moles, and birthmarks are completely normal, though some girls feel self-conscious about them. These are just spots where your skin has a different amount of *melanin*, a pigment that determines skin color.

As you grow, you might notice thin lines called *stretch marks* on your skin or textured areas called *cellulite*, especially on your thighs, stomach, breasts, and upper arms. Many girls also have scars from getting hurt or having surgery. All these markings are completely normal and nothing to be ashamed of.

More than skin-deep

It's a tough reality that people make assumptions about others based on how dark or light their skin is. If you're a girl of color, you might feel left out in spaces where no one else looks like you. You might even face poor treatment sometimes. At the same time, your skin can help you feel proud of who you are and the community you belong to. In your skin and in your heart, you carry the legacy of your ancestors, and that's something to be proud of. You deserve to love the skin you're in.

You can't tell someone's race just by their skin color. Though skin color is coded in your genes, race isn't. Race is an idea that humans came up with to categorize people into groups. Skin color varies a lot, even among people of the same race.

I'm Black, and I love playing with makeup. But when I follow tutorials, my makeup never turns out the same as the person's in the video. It's like they're only for people with light skin, which makes me feel kind of bad about myself. Got any advice?

Leah, Wisconsin

It can be frustrating to see a look you really like on someone else and have it turn out totally different when you try it yourself. But remember, your skin color is something to celebrate! Look for tutorials by people with a skin tone similar to yours. They can share the products and techniques that are perfect for your beautiful hue. The only videos worth watching are ones that make you feel great about yourself!

Real Girl RUNWAY

Zoe T. empowers girls of color to love their skin

Zoe was five when she first faced bullying for her skin color and hair texture. "It made me feel really bad," Zoe says. "It made me feel like I couldn't do anything." One thing that helped her feel better was playing with her Black dolls. Zoe knew her dolls were beautiful, which reminded her that she was beautiful, too.

To help other girls love themselves, Zoe started collecting Black and Brown dolls and donating them to girls in need. She called her organization Zoe's Dolls. So far, she's donated over 32,000 dolls!

As Zoe got older, her interests changed—and so did her activism! Through Zoe's Dolls, she organized new programs to help empower girls of color. For example, Loving the Skin I'm In gives girls a chance to create encouraging poems and videos about why they love their unique selves. She's even starting a podcast about Black girl empowerment and social justice! "My voice is changing, and I want to share that with the rest of my community," Zoe says.

Through the years, one thing hasn't changed: Zoe's motto for life. At every Zoe's Dolls event, she asks everyone to stand and repeat these words:

❝ I am beautiful! I am powerful! I am LOVE! ❞

"These are powerful words," Zoe says. "I want everyone to really feel the words and know they're true." 25

awesome and able

Having a body that looks, moves, and communicates differently than others can affect your body image. Your difference might be noticeable, like if you have cerebral palsy and use a wheelchair, walker, or crutches to get around. Or, you might have a difference that's not very noticeable at all, like asthma. It's totally normal to worry about your body having unique needs or looking different than other bodies. Remember that your body is worthy and good, just as it is.

How is your body different from other bodies? Have those differences ever made you feel ashamed? Have they ever made you feel proud or strong?

All bodies are good bodies, no matter which adaptive equipment, medicine, or special assistance they need. You deserve to feel included and comfortable in your classroom and the places you go outside of school. If you don't—for example, if you find yourself in a two-story building without an elevator or in a movie theater without closed-captioning devices—it's not your body's fault. It's the fault of the people who designed the space without bodies like yours in mind.

Sitting like this hurts. Will the other kids think I'm faking it if I ask to move?

I'm glad my body reminds me when it's time to take a break.

PARTS OF A CELL

The Americans with Disabilities Act, or ADA, is a law that strives to remove barriers so everyone can access schools, businesses, museums, and websites. Thanks to the ADA, public spaces are required to have parking spaces, ramps, and bathrooms designed with disabled bodies in mind. While not every space is accessible yet, many activists—like Judy Heumann and Alice Wong—are working hard to ensure that the future is accessible for everyone.

Remember, your body is not a problem or a burden. Your body is worthy, valid, and good. All bodies are.

Can-do attitude

Studies show that focusing on what your body lets you experience instead of what it looks like can improve your body image. Can your body . . .

hear beautiful sounds?

laugh at a funny joke?

All bodies have different abilities, and all bodies can do awesome things.

plant flowers and watch them grow?

Make a list of all the things your body can do. The longer the list, the better! Use these prompts to get started.

My body can use its senses to . . .

- watch sunsets.
- smell cookies baking in the oven.
- feel a soft blanket.
- 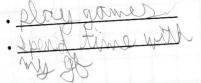 play games
- spend time with my gf

With my body, I can express myself by . . .

- singing.
- drawing a picture.
- telling stories with my friends.
- _____
- _____

My body can move by . . .

- bending and stretching.
- dancing.
- swimming.
- 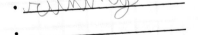 running
- _____

My body helps me reach my goals by . . .

- learning new things in school.
- taking me to new, exciting places.
- practicing new skills until I master them.
- _____
- _____

My body keeps me healthy by . . .

- keeping my heart pumping.
- sleeping when I need rest.
- cooling me off with sweat when I get hot.
- growing new skin when I get a cut.
- _____
- _____

growing and flowing

One of the most amazing things your body does is GROW! The time when your body develops and changes the most is called *puberty*, and for most girls it starts between ages 8 and 13. And puberty doesn't just change your body—it can transform your body image, too. Learning what to expect can help you trust your body and feel good about yourself during these changes.

Bigger and better

At some point, usually around age 9 or 10, most girls experience a growth spurt. Every body grows a little differently. You could grow fast when you're young and stop growing before other girls even begin their growth spurts. Or maybe you'll have your growth spurt much later, surprising your friends in high school by becoming a tall teenager. You might also start tall and stay tall or start small and stay small.

I've been really stressed about my height. All of my friends are over 5 feet, and I'm only 4 feet, 10 inches. It makes me mad, and I cry a lot. I have Turner syndrome, which will make me even shorter than other girls. I need advice.

Clarissa, Missouri

Growing up isn't a race, and when it comes to height, every girl is different. Comparing your body to your friends just sets you up to feel terrible! Girls with Turner syndrome, or any kind of genetic difference, need to give their bodies kindness just like anyone going through puberty. Listen to your doctor's advice about treatment options and caring for your body. Besides that, all you can do is be you! Celebrate the things that your perfect, short body can do.

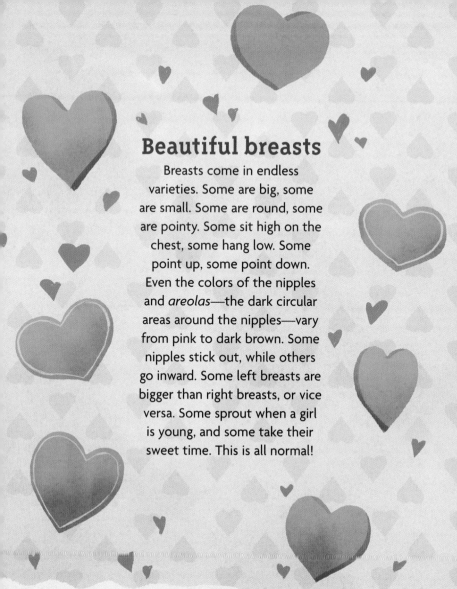

Beautiful breasts

Breasts come in endless varieties. Some are big, some are small. Some are round, some are pointy. Some sit high on the chest, some hang low. Some point up, some point down. Even the colors of the nipples and *areolas*—the dark circular areas around the nipples—vary from pink to dark brown. Some nipples stick out, while others go inward. Some left breasts are bigger than right breasts, or vice versa. Some sprout when a girl is young, and some take their sweet time. This is all normal!

I have big boobs for my age, but the one thing I don't like about them is that they sag! They just don't look the way boobs should look, and I'm nervous about it. Will my boobs be like this forever?
Erika, North Dakota

If you've seen breasts in movies, you might get the idea that they're supposed to be big, round, and perky. But it's very rare for women to naturally have breasts that look that way. Hello, Hollywood, have you heard of gravity? Many boobs sag, especially when they're on the bigger side. And just like your body size, your genes are pretty much in charge of what your breasts look like—you don't have control over it. The best thing to do is find a supportive bra that you feel comfortable in.

Hair today, more tomorrow

During puberty, hair starts showing up in places you might not have noticed before—on your arms and legs, in your armpits and pubic area, and even on your face. This hair can make you feel self-conscious, but there's nothing dirty or wrong about it. Many girls and women decide to remove hair from certain areas of their bodies, while others prefer to leave it alone. Removing hair is a very personal choice, and you should only do it if it feels right for your body (and after talking to a parent).

I'm 10, and I have really dark hair on my legs. I'm embarrassed to wear shorts to school or in public. I just tell my friends my mom won't let me wear shorts until June 1st. I want to shave, but I'm scared. Do you have any solutions?

Skylar, Kentucky

If you're scared to shave, you're probably not ready. And that's OK! It's your body, and you (with the help of an adult) get to decide if and when shaving is right for you. But avoiding shorts when it's warm out is going to be tough! Remember that loving your body means appreciating it for what it can do, not what it looks like. Challenge yourself to wear the right clothes for your favorite summer activities, even if it means exposing your legs. If you catch someone staring, say, "Shaving is a big deal, and I'm just not ready."

I'm good-looking and I get good grades in my classes. But there's a problem. I have a mustache. Well, not like those thick mustaches you see on men, but still. I'm the only one of my friends who has one. Boys bully me about it, and I'm afraid to tell my teacher. Is there anything I can do to make it go away? It makes me feel self-conscious! Help!

Abigail, New York

It's totally normal for girls to have upper lip hair, though it's easier to notice if you have dark hair and light or medium skin. There's nothing wrong with it, and you never have to remove it if you don't want to. If bullies point it out, shrug and say, "So?" and go on with your life. And don't hesitate to tell your teacher, parent, or a guidance counselor about the bullying. They can help put a stop to it. In the meantime, hold your head high and remind yourself that you deserve to love yourself, facial hair and all.

Acne

During puberty, your skin creates more oils, which can lead to acne. It's totally normal, and there's nothing dirty or ugly about it. You don't need to buy expensive creams and scrubs to take care of your skin. The best thing you can do is to wash your face with a gentle soap, pat dry, and then apply a light moisturizer. Besides that, keep your hands off!

I am nine years old, and I have about 30 zits! I watched millions of videos about how to get rid of zits, but no luck. Also, I'm about to go to a new school, and my face is going to be messed up!

Bella, Rhode Island

Even if you do a great job with your skin-care routine, you're bound to still have pimples. Plus, a stressful event like starting at a new school can make a breakout worse. To help calm your body, take slow, deep breaths throughout the day and before bed. Then on your first day at school, wear an outfit that makes you feel like a million bucks. Chances are, your new classmates will see your confidence, not your pimples.

Go with the flow

Starting your period can have a big impact on your body image. It might make one girl feel proud and grown-up. It might make another feel scared and confused, or even ashamed. Remember, periods are normal. There is *nothing* to be ashamed of.

A lot of girls worry that they'll start too early or too late. But your body knows what it's doing! All you can do is go with the flow, because there's no way to slow it down or speed it up. Instead, focus on showing love to your body with food, exercise, plenty of rest, and good hygiene.

GO WITH THE FLOW

I feel really weird because I'm only 11 and already have my period. Most girls at my school have barely even started developing breasts. I've also noticed that boys have started acting weird around me. Somehow me having my period got spread around the school and now every time I walk past a boy, they start whispering about me.

Ellie, Washington

Comparing your body to others is a really bad idea. You started puberty at exactly the time that was right for your body—there's no way you could've stopped it. It doesn't mean that you're more mature or that you can't do the same fun things you've always done. As for the boys whispering about you, that sounds humiliating. No one deserves to have their body discussed and looked at like that. Tell an adult, like a parent or teacher, so they can help put a stop to it.

Dare to not compare

Comparing yourself to others can push you to be a better person. If your friend Ciara reads 45 books over the summer, you might decide to read 50. Or seeing your cousin Levi help out at the food pantry every Saturday might inspire you to volunteer, too. Comparing what you do with what others do can be helpful.

But comparing your *body* to someone else's is a recipe for bad body image. Let's say you're the only girl in your class with glasses, and you wish for perfect eyesight like everyone else. Does that comparison help you become a better person? Nope. It just makes you feel bad about something you can't control.

Pay attention when a body comparison creeps into your mind. Is it helpful or hurtful? Even if you can't stop the thought, realizing that it's a hurtful comparison can help you keep it quiet and get on with your day.

Comparison		Helpful?

Comparison	Helpful?
Why haven't I started my period yet? Everyone else I know has!	**No.** My body is changing at its own pace.
My hair is as straight as a stick. I want bouncy curls like Sasha!	**Not really.** It's fun to use a curling iron on special occasions, but my hair is what it is.
No one else has pimples as bad as mine. My face is one giant, fiery blister.	**No and yes.** If you're already washing and moisturizing your face, there's no use beating yourself up about pimples. Some girls get a lot of them and others don't. But if you're in a lot of pain, it might be time to see a doctor to help you feel better.

35

gender joy

Messages about how bodies "should" look are different depending on a person's gender. Girls tend to face more pressure to have thin bodies and long hair and to wear clothes like skirts, dresses, and blouses. Boys tend to feel more pressure to have a muscular body, keep their hair short, and wear pants and shorts. Luckily, it's not your job to look the way people expect—it's your job to be you.

The way you show your gender to the world through clothes and behaviors is your *gender expression*. Your gender expression can be feminine, masculine, or somewhere in between—and it might change! Maybe you'll experiment with bright dresses and long, feminine hairstyles. Or you might try baggy shorts, plaid shirts, and a buzzed haircut. Your gender expression should make you feel at home in your body.

While gender expression is what you show on the outside, *gender identity* is how you feel on the inside—a girl, a boy, or someone who doesn't quite fit into either category. When a baby is born, a doctor looks at the baby's body parts to assign its *sex*—whether the baby is female or male. Most kids grow up feeling comfortable in the sex the doctor assigned. This kind of person is *cisgender*. (Say it *sis-jen-dur*.) But for some, that assigned sex doesn't match who they know they are inside. A kid who was assigned as male might know herself to be a girl inside, for example. Someone whose gender is different than the sex they were assigned at birth is *transgender*. Some people don't feel like a girl *or* a boy inside—which is totally OK! People in this group are usually called *nonbinary* and might use a pronoun like *they* instead of *he* or *she*.

Being transgender is not an illness or something to be ashamed of. If you're questioning your gender identity—or if you already know for sure that you're trans or nonbinary—talk with an adult you trust, like a parent or school counselor. That person can connect you with a specially trained doctor, who can help you and your family decide what's best for your body. At first, you and the doctor might talk about wearing the clothes and using the pronouns (like *he*, *she*, or *they*) that make you feel most like the true you. If you haven't gone through puberty yet, the doctor might offer medicine to delay your body's changes, giving you more time to think about your gender identity. And if you've already gone through puberty, a doctor can still help. Studies show that transgender and nonbinary kids who get help from doctors have much better mental health than those who don't.

If you don't have an adult you trust, there are organizations across the country that can help you. Turn to the Resources on page 95 for more information.

> Being transgender isn't a medical transition. It's a process of learning to love yourself for who you are.
>
> —Jazz Jennings

If you're transgender or nonbinary, loving your body might feel a bit different than it does for a cisgender person. Parts of your body might make you feel uncomfortable, and you might want to change the way you look. That's totally OK! You can appreciate your body for everything it allows you to experience and still want to change certain things about it. When you're feeling out of place in your body, do things that make your body feel more like home, like dressing in your favorite clothes and doing something you love. Celebrate the good feelings you have in your body right now. Remember, you deserve love and respect, no matter what your body looks like or how it changes.

body image in distress

Some illnesses affect your body, like ear infections or chicken pox. But there are also illnesses that affect your body *image*. These are mental health conditions, which means they involve your thinking and behavior. Having one is not your fault. And like any illness, it might require help from a doctor.

Body dysmorphia

Most girls worry about their appearance every now and then. But for girls with *body dysmorphia*, that worry starts taking over their lives. The illness causes them to obsess over an aspect of their body they dislike, such as their nose, skin, tummy, or breasts. Other people rarely even notice this feature of the girl's body. Still, girls spend hours every day evaluating the body part or covering it up. They might stop spending time with friends and family, pursuing hobbies, playing sports, and even going to school. It can be serious, and it doesn't go away on its own.

Disordered eating and eating disorders

A poor body image can lead to unhealthy changes in the way you eat. *Disordered eating* is an approach to food that focuses on changing the way your body looks, not keeping it healthy. Girls with disordered eating might go on diets, skip meals, and obsessively count calories but also feel out of control around food. Disordered eating can be hard to spot because it often looks like "super healthy" eating. But it's not healthy, and it can lead to even more dangerous issues.

When disordered eating is severe enough, it becomes an *eating disorder*. There are three main types:

- *Anorexia* causes a girl to starve herself. To lose weight, she might eat only very small meals, skip meals altogether, or exercise until she's exhausted. She can develop serious heart problems, thinning bones, hair loss, and digestion issues. If she doesn't get help, anorexia might cause her body to start shutting down.

- Girls with *bulimia* eat large amounts of food at one time (called *bingeing*) and then try to get rid of it (called *purging*) to keep their bodies from gaining weight. During purging, a girl might force herself to vomit, use laxatives to make herself poop, or exercise until she's exhausted.

- *Binge eating disorder* is similar to bulimia and causes girls to eat a large amount of food at one time, even when they're not hungry. They often feel ashamed afterward but don't purge the food from their bodies.

Anyone can get an eating disorder, and you can't tell whether someone has one by looking at them. Eating disorders tend to affect girls more than boys, and they usually start in late elementary school, middle school, or high school.

Getting help for yourself

If you think you might be struggling with body dysmorphia or an eating disorder, remember that *it's not your fault*. Some girls don't seek help because they're embarrassed or don't think they have a real problem. But these conditions don't go away on their own. Talk to your parents or another adult you trust so you can get the treatment you need. Don't suffer alone—this problem is too big for any girl to tackle by herself.

Getting help for a friend

Watching a friend suffer with these issues is tough. Here are some ways to help:

- Express your concerns in a loving way. Remind her that having this condition isn't her fault and that you care about her no matter what.

- Stick to statements that start with "I" instead of "you" to show your friend that you're not blaming her for the problem. For example, instead of saying, "You don't eat lunch anymore," try saying, "I've noticed you don't eat lunch anymore."

- Never tell her to simply "get over it" or just "start eating normally again." It's not that easy, and your advice could be hurtful.

- Encourage your friend to tell an adult what's going on. Recovering from body dysmorphia or an eating disorder isn't easy, and your friend can't do it alone. If she refuses to get help, tell an adult you trust.

the one and only you

Part of developing a healthy body image is honoring each and every piece of you. Look at the palm of your hand. See all the intersecting lines? Imagine each of those lines represents one piece of your gender, race, ability, religion, where you're from, and everything else that makes you *you*. No one else has a pattern quite like yours.

If you look at just *one* of those lines, you're not seeing the whole you. No one is *just* a girl. No one is *just* someone with a learning disability. No one is *just* a person whose parents immigrated from China. Everyone is made up of many, many identities that intersect in unique ways. This way of looking at your identity is called *intersectionality*. Intersectionality helps you celebrate your uniqueness as well as examine the things that make it easier or harder for your body to move through the world.

What does your identity look like?

Race:
_____

Gender:
_____

Age:
_____

Cisgender or transgender:
_____

Place you were born:
_____

Disabled or nondisabled:
_____

Gender expression:
_____

Language you speak at home:
_____

Thin, wide, or average body:
_____

Short, tall, or average height:
_____

Real Girl RUNWAY

Intersectional Ivy

10-year-old Ivy G. is Deaf, transgender, and Jewish, and her first language is American Sign Language (ASL). But those identities are just the beginning. She also loves unicorns, llamas, cheerleading, fashion, painting, putting on her mom's red lipstick, playing video games, baking cookies, meeting with other Deaf trans youth, and making the world a better place for everyone.

Intersectionality is important to Ivy because there's no way she can move through the world as *just* a Deaf person or *just* a transgender girl. She's both—plus a lot more! "Intersectionality means that every single part that's in me, from my toes to my head, makes me *me*," Ivy says.

Ivy is proud to be who she is. Still, she sometimes has bad days. To feel better, she draws, polishes her toenails, or talks to her best friend, Molly, who's been there for Ivy since before she told people she was transgender.

When Ivy first came out to people at her school for Deaf students, people didn't understand what it meant to be transgender. So her mom encouraged her to create videos to educate people using ASL. Now people understand better. Ivy's videos also help people in the transgender community better understand Deaf people. Her mission is to make space for *everyone* at the table.

> Everyone should be themselves and be comfortable as who they are.
>
> —Ivy

LOVE YOUR BODY

eat

Eating food seems like a no-brainer. But spend five minutes researching "how to eat healthy," and you'll find a bottomless pit of contradicting information, shady advice, and flashy ads for the latest diet.

Eating shouldn't be complicated. The best way to love your body is to stick to the basics.

NEW MESSAGE

Honor your body's hunger signals. Your body sends messages to your brain when you're hungry, thirsty, or full. All you have to do is pay attention. You don't need to count calories or calculate the grams of fat on your plate. Your body isn't a math problem to solve!

Stick to a schedule. Your body is happiest when you eat breakfast, lunch, dinner, and snacks around the same time every day. A schedule reminds your body that when it's hungry, more food is coming soon. You'll feel more energized, focused, and comfortable throughout the day.

Eat healthy food that's delicious. Do you force yourself to eat raw kale just to get your healthy eating over with for the day? That sounds terrible! If you train your body to love—truly love—veggies and fruits, you're more likely to eat them. Experiment with different spices and preparation styles, like squash in a curry, bell peppers on the grill, or crispy kale sprinkled with salt. Ask your family if you can get involved with meal planning so you can make sure there's always something healthy and yummy for dinner!

Keep treats on the menu. Many people cut out sweets and "junk" food when they're trying to eat healthy. But studies show that putting these foods off-limits actually makes you eat even more of them! Instead of banishing treats, simply listen to your body's cues about how much of them to eat.

I can't stop eating junk food. Whenever I get home from school, I lie down and eat a box of cheese crackers while doing homework. Got any advice?

Lily, Florida

Eating a snack when you get home from school is a great way to give your body the energy it needs between lunch and dinner. But it's hard to listen to your body's signals when you're concentrating on homework. Instead, set aside time for a snack before you start working, and make it an enjoyable time to look forward to. Experiment with different snacks like celery with peanut butter or apples with cheese to see which foods help you concentrate best.

diet? don't try it!

Over half of girls in middle school have dieted to lose weight in the last year. But scientists have known for decades that diets don't work! Ninety-five percent of people who go on a diet—any diet at all—don't actually lose weight. In fact, studies show that people who go on diets actually gain more weight than those who don't. Yep, you read that right. One reason is that dieting can slow down your metabolism—your body's way of turning food into fuel.

Diet can mean the type of food someone usually eats. For example, you might say, "I try to eat a healthy diet by including a vegetable at every meal," or "My cat eats a diet of kibble and tuna treats." But in this book, when we say diet, we're talking about a way of restricting food, usually to lose weight.

Diets don't work because they force you to ignore your body's hunger messages.

Healthy eating: I listen to my body and give it as much food as it needs. I don't put certain foods off-limits—I eat what makes me feel good.

Dieting: I follow a diet plan to tell me how much food my body needs. As long as I have enough self-control to ignore my cravings, I can stick to the foods that will help me lose weight.

The Diet Cycle

Starting a diet can thrust you into a never-ending loop that does your body much more harm than good.

Start

My body needs to change. You're not feeling great about your body, so you start a diet. Even if you know that diets don't work, you think to yourself, "As long as I stay strong, I can beat the odds."

I can do this.
You ignore your body's hunger signals and cravings and stick to your diet plan. You might lose a little weight (or you might not). Meanwhile, your body assumes that you're starving and begins Operation Keep You Alive. That means slowing down and burning fewer calories than normal.

I'm so hungry.
Your body screams at you to eat the delicious foods that you haven't had in a while. You feel grumpy and might not have as much energy as usual. If you play sports, your performance declines, even if you're working harder than ever. You think about food *all the time*.

I'm ashamed.
Your body image plummets, and you feel like a total failure. If you lost weight, it comes back— plus a few extra pounds. Having a body you love starts to feel impossible.

I need food!
The hunger signals become so strong that you finally eat the food your body has been asking for. And most likely, you eat *a lot* of it. Meanwhile, your body throws a party because it finally has the fuel it needs! Just in case it has to live through another dry spell, it stores as much fat as possible. (This is why dieting causes people to gain weight in the long run, not lose it.)

It's hard to escape the diet cycle once you're in it. But the most important thing to remember is that *it's not your fault*. Diet and exercise companies *want* you to fall into this cycle. That way as you get older you'll spend money on expensive diet plans, food, and exercise videos, again and again. The best way to break the cycle is to stop punishing your body and start listening to it.

49

step away from the scale

A number on a scale doesn't tell you anything about your health, but it can do a great job of ruining your day.

If you have a scale at home, talk to your parents about getting rid of it or putting it somewhere out of sight. (Scales aren't good for an adult's body image either!) If they say no, write a positive message on a sticky note and press it over the numbers.

Why are you weighed during a check-up? Doctors use many different criteria—including weight—to help make sure your body is growing at a healthy rate. If there's a big jump or drop in your weight, your doctor might want to investigate why. But unless your doctor tells you to weigh yourself at home to monitor a specific health problem, there's no reason to.

winner winner, family dinner

Studies show that kids who eat dinner with their families develop healthier eating habits and more positive body image and even do better in school. Whether family dinner means sitting down to a home-cooked meal with your parents, heating up leftovers with your siblings while your mom is at work, or squeezing in a takeout meal before softball practice, the important thing is to connect with the people around you. Turn off the TV, put away the phones, and talk to each other.

Here are some mealtime questions to get the conversation going:

If you could teach a class about any subject, what would it be?

What new tradition would you create for our family?

What's the funniest thing that happened to you today?

If you had your human body but any animal's head, which animal would you choose?

How would you spend your perfect day?

If you could suddenly have any talent, what would it be?

How do you know someone will be a good friend?

If your pet could talk, what would it say?

If you could have any book character as a best friend, who would it be?

51

move it!

No matter what size or shape your body is or what your abilities are, moving your body is healthy! Exercising . . .

builds strong bones.

strengthens your muscles.

gives you energy throughout the day.

helps your heart.

improves your sleep.

boosts your self-confidence.

soothes your stress and boosts your mood.

helps you concentrate at school.

1h

Experts agree that girls your age should get at least one hour of physical activity every day. That can include everything from going to soccer practice, to racing scooters in gym class, to walking your dog. Even moving your body a few days per week boosts your mental health.

Just like with eating, it's important to listen to your body. If you dread exercise, or if you move your body only to make it look different, it's time to find some new activities. Your best friend might love running 5K races. But if the thought of running makes you want to hide under your bed, it's not the exercise for you! Try other movements—shooting hoops, dancing in your bedroom, climbing trees, challenging your brother to a push-up contest—anything that makes you feel good.

About a third of kids drop out of sports every year, especially starting around fifth grade. The biggest reason: Sports stop being fun. It's so important to find ways to exercise that you truly enjoy.

What if my body has to look a certain way for my sport?

If you participate in dance, gymnastics, figure skating, or swimming, you might run into extra pressure to be thin. One study of high school girls in these sports showed that over 40 percent struggled with disordered eating. These girls were eight times more likely than their peers to get injured because their bodies weren't getting the right nutrition.

You should *never* have to change the way your body looks to do an activity you love. It feels terrible when others judge and scrutinize your body, especially while you're wearing a tight uniform. But as an athlete, your job is to focus on how your body *works*, not how it looks. Trying to force your body into a certain shape doesn't make it work better—it makes you weaker and more prone to injury.

53

Real Girl RUNWAY

Kinley A.
Kills It on the Dance Floor

When 12-year-old Kinley starts dancing, nothing can stop her. "Dancing puts me in my happy place," she says.

She started dancing ballet when she was two, but it was too slow and boring for her. At age four, she found her passion: hip-hop. "I practice literally every day, all day, until my sisters tell me to PLEASE SIT DOWN," Kinley says.

Kinley has faced bullying in the past, and she's heard plenty of rude comments about her body size. People don't expect her to be a good dancer—but she can demolish anyone in a dance-off. She's won many freestyle dance battles and scholarships, and she even got to do a dance-off against tWitch, one of her favorite hip-hop dancers of all time.

Kinley keeps a positive attitude about her body and the amazing things it can do. "I love that my body is unique," she says. Still, she does have days when she struggles with her body image. She has severe asthma, and the medicine she takes can affect her weight. But dancing helps her feel great about herself again.

"When I'm dancing, nothing else matters but my next move," Kinley says.

54

month of movement challenge

2 JANUARY

1 JANUARY

BODY IMAGE BOOST

For one month, move your body in at least one different way every single day. Check off the ideas below as you try them and add plenty of your own! You might find a fun way to exercise that you've never thought of before. Ready, set, GO!

☐ Design an obstacle course with chairs, blankets, and paper towel tubes.

☐ Sit on the floor, bend your knees, and lift your legs. Now pull yourself up with an invisible rope, and imagine you're scaling a skyscraper.

☐ Pretend the floor is lava.

☐ Toss a disc with a friend.

☐ Try a sport you've never played before, like tennis, pickleball, juggling, or paddleboarding.

☐ Grab a friend and a camera with a timer. Set the camera to take a picture every 10 seconds. With your bodies, spell out every letter of the alphabet and get a picture of each one.

☐ Blow up a balloon and bounce it in the air as long as you can.

If you have a disability that makes it hard to play certain sports, you might enjoy joining an adaptive sports program. Adaptive sports use special equipment and rules to make games fun for people with bodies that work differently than others. Ask a grown-up to search online for adaptive sports in your area to find out what's available.

☐ Have a dance-off with a friend.

☐ Ask a parent to help you find a beginning yoga video online, and give it a try!

☐ Have a water balloon or snowball fight.

☐ Start a four-square tournament with your neighbors.

☐ Create a treasure hunt for a friend and go with her as she solves it. Then ask her to make a treasure hunt for you.

☐ Hold a kickball between your knees and see how far you can hop without dropping it.

☐ Twirl a fitness hoop as long as you can. Then beat that time.

☐ Rake leaves or weed a garden.

☐ Explore a hiking trail.

▲ HIKE

☐ Climb a grassy hill and roll down it.

☐ Draw a hopscotch court with 30 squares.

Wear a helmet whenever you ride your bike, skateboard, scooter, or skates. Loving your body means protecting it from injuries!

Do you have trouble fitting your hair inside a helmet? Try putting your hair in a low bun or braiding it into two plaits that lie flat against your head. You can also put on a silk bonnet or headscarf to give your hair extra protection.

☐ Ride your bike.

56

you're the boss of your body

Your body belongs to you, and no one else. Eating and exercising are two ways you get to take charge of your body. But being the boss of your body also means:

- Asking for *consent* (permission) before touching people and expecting others to do the same for you. Some people love hugs, others prefer high-fives, and others don't like being touched at all. No one should assume that it's OK to touch you unless you say it's OK.

- Accepting only touch that feels good. If someone touches you in a way you like, such as giving you a shoulder massage, you can say, "Wow, that feels really nice!" On the other hand, if someone touches you in a way that hurts or makes you uncomfortable, firmly say "that's enough" or "please stop now." Even if you give your consent for someone to touch you, you can take it away at any time, for any reason.

- Get comfortable saying no. As you get older, you'll face pressure to make choices you know are wrong, like drinking alcohol, vaping or smoking, or taking drugs. If you know something isn't healthy for your body, it's your job to keep it out.

57

dress to express

Clothes cover our bodies and keep us warm. But clothes can also say to the world, "This is who I am!" Wearing clothes that make you feel like you is a great way to boost your body confidence. Here's how:

Wear colors, patterns, and styles that make you feel awesome. Are you a tie-dye and rainbows girl? Do cheetah-print dresses call to you? Or are button-down shirts and bow ties more your style? Choosing styles you love helps the true you shine.

Wear clothes that fit. A waistband digging into your belly or a shirt that rides up is a total confidence killer. Your body deserves to be comfortable and take up all the space it needs.

Focus on you. Do you want those expensive black leggings because you love them or because the most popular girl at school has three pairs? You'll never find your style if you're looking for it in someone else's wardrobe.

Dress for the occasion.
Going for a hike? You'll probably need some sturdy shoes and a hat. Going to a fancy dinner party at the mayor's house? You'll probably want to leave your glow-in-the-dark dinosaur suit at home (unless it's a costume party, of course!). Plan ahead so you can always be comfortable in what you're wearing.

Work with what you have.
Just because you spot the perfect lime-green jumpsuit doesn't mean you can afford it. But don't let a small budget stop you from expressing your style! Visit thrift stores and garage sales to find unique pieces. And look online with a parent for do-it-yourself videos about restyling old clothes into new looks.

If you could wear *any* outfit to show off the true you, what would it be? What's holding you back from wearing it?

What you wear can change how you feel inside. In one study, scientists found that when people put on a white doctor's coat, they completed tasks more accurately. That's because the white coats made them feel smarter and more capable, like a doctor. So choose clothes that make you feel smart, confident, and uniquely you!

I am very big for my age, and I have trouble finding clothes I like. My mom doesn't really get it, and it's very awkward talking to her about it. I don't know what to do.

Adelaide, North Carolina

Having a closet full of clothes that you dislike is tough. The frustrating truth is that clothing brands don't offer as many options for bigger bodies as they do for thin bodies. And the options they do offer are often . . . well, let's just say grandma-ish. (No offense, Grandma.) But you deserve to feel *great* in the clothes you wear. Read that again.

First, have a talk with your mom about how your clothes make you feel. You could say, "Mom, I want to feel confident at school. I think some different clothes could really make a difference." Then do some online research together for plus-size clothing brands. Though stores in your town might not have cute clothes in your size, you'll find a lot more options online.

Find clothes designed with your body in mind.

More and more brands are creating clothes for a wide variety of bodies. For example, adaptive brands design clothes that fit people with various disabilities and make getting dressed easier. And if you love a brand but can't find clothes that work for your body, consider writing a letter to the company. Chances are, you're not the only one who has this problem!

Real Girl RUNWAY

Fearless Fatima

Sometimes clothes are more than just clothes. That's true for Fatima A., who covers her hair with a *hijab*, a headscarf. Fatima's hijab represents her Muslim identity and connects her to her community. It's not just something she wears—it's part of who she is.

When Fatima was 12, she flew to her first international competition for the US Squash Junior National Team. (Squash is a sport played with rackets and a tiny ball.) But before she could get on the plane, an airline worker demanded that she take off her hijab to verify her identity.

Fatima was horrified. She explained that she needed to keep her scarf on for religious reasons, but the man wouldn't let her on the plane until she removed it. Fatima was determined not to take off her hijab in public, even if it meant missing the flight and the tournament. But she agreed to take it off in a corner with a female airline agent. It was humiliating, especially because she wasn't allowed to go to a private room.

> "Taking it off isn't just like taking off your sock," Fatima said later. "It's almost like taking off a limb. It's a big deal to me. It's part of my Muslim identity and who I am as a person. So when someone tells me to just casually take it off and hurry up, it's degrading."

Fatima and her family let the airline know how hurtful Fatima's experience was. Because they spoke up, the airline apologized and changed its rules so that something like this never happens again. Fatima wants all people who wear religious head coverings to feel proud and safe when they travel.

makeup and more

Experimenting with makeup, jewelry, nail polish, and hairstyles is a great way to discover your unique style. Just keep these big, important points in mind:

Get permission first. Some parents are OK with makeup, some might allow it only on special days, and others say, "not under my roof!" It can be frustrating when your parents don't see things from your point of view, but remember that they have your best interests in mind. They might worry about you looking too grown-up or starting a beauty routine that will cost a lot of time and money in the long run. Each family has different values when it comes to makeup, nails, and hair, and it's important to honor that.

You do you, girl! Girls face a lot of pressure to look like other girls, and that goes for hair and makeup styles, too. But it's not your job to buy the same shade of lip gloss as every girl in your school—it's your job to be you! When you find yourself looking at a beauty product and saying, "I *have* to have this," think again. If you'd never seen another girl wear it or use it, would you feel the same way?

It's all optional. Makeup, nail polish, and fancy hairstyles are never required for going to school, hanging out with friends, or leaving the house. Your body has the right to exist in the world with or without decorations.

I love painting my nails and trying out new colors and designs. The problem is, I'm not allowed to wear nail polish until I'm 13, which to me sounds dumb. My parents only let me wear it once in a while. I feel like I'm being treated like a baby! How can I convince my parents I'm not too young (without arguing or snipping back)?

Arwyn, New Hampshire

It's tough to feel like you can't express yourself the way you want to. Try having a calm conversation with your parents about what nail polish means to you—that it's not about looking like other girls but about showing the world your unique self. But if your parents still say no, that's final. While you wait to turn 13, find other ways to express yourself. Can you wear bold, sparkly necklaces that match your outfits? Can you experiment with a new hairstyle and colorful accessories? Painting your nails is just one of the many, many ways you can show off who you are.

bounce back

All this body image pressure can be overwhelming sometimes. You're not going to feel great about your body every single day. But there are ways to build your *resilience*—your ability to bounce back from tough feelings or events. Here's how:

Work on something you're good at. It can be anything from sculpting clay animals, to practicing hard at your favorite sport, to growing plants on your windowsill. Feeling confident about your abilities helps you bounce back when you're feeling down.

Connect with friends, family, classmates, teammates, neighbors, and people in your community. Having people you can rely on when things get tough is one of the best ways to be resilient.

Be a role model for others. Do your best, treat others with respect, and make the choices you know are right even when they're difficult.

Put good into the world. Volunteer, join a social justice club, or help a friend in need. The good vibes you send out will come back to you when you're having a tough day.

BODY IMAGE BOOST

quick fixes

Sometimes you need a way to feel better *right now*.
Here are some quick ways to jump-start your body image:

Take a nap.

Go for a walk.

Bend over, letting your arms dangle. Take a deep breath, in and out. Sweeping your arms out to each side, stand up and point your fingers to the sky. Stretch out as tall as you can! Release your arms, and fold your body in half again.

Scream into a pillow.

Video-chat a friend.

If you've recently skipped a meal, eat.

Smell something delightful, like your favorite lotion or a scented candle.

Take a shower.

Do a relaxing craft, like coloring in a coloring book or making a friendship bracelet.

Listen to your favorite song.

Write down how you're feeling in a journal.

Declutter your sleeping or homework area. A clean space can help you breathe a little easier.

Massage your left hand with your right hand. Then switch.

Laugh. Check out your favorite funny videos or make the silliest face you can in the mirror.

Read a book.

Cuddle with a pet or stuffed animal.

65

THE BACKGROUND ON BEAUTY

The Birth of Venus
Sandro Botticelli, 1482
Italy

Beautiful Bodies through the Ages

Venus of Willendorf
Unknown artist,
30,000 BCE
Austria

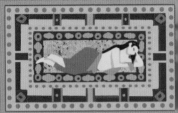

A Young Lady Reclining After a Bath
Muhammad Mumin, 1590s
Afghanistan

Self-Portrait with the Portrait of Doctor Farill
Frida Kahlo, 1951
Mexico

Venus at a Mirror
Peter Paul Rubens, 1615
Belgium

All Things Bright and Beautiful
Amy Sherald, 2016
United States

Female figure
Unknown Baule artist, 1800s
Côte d'Ivoire

what's beauty?

Close your eyes and imagine a painting of a beautiful girl. How is her body shaped? How tall is she? What kind of hair does she have? What color is her skin?

For the most part, ideas about beauty come from images in the media—art, magazines, movies, videos, TV, billboards, social platforms, and advertisements. It's called a *beauty standard,* society's definition of what a person "should" look like. A beauty standard isn't about health. It's not about feeling good or having strong character. It's just about how a person looks.

Beauty standards change all the time. If you lived in tenth-century China, "beautiful" would bring to mind a pale face, dramatic eyebrows, thin lips, and tiny feet. In sixteenth-century Italy, you'd probably imagine a plump woman with pale skin and plenty of curves. And in Fiji in the 1900s, you'd think of a woman with brown skin who's robust and strong.

Which beauty standard is right? In short, none of them. Beauty standards tell girls and women that they need to change their appearance depending on what's in style. But your body isn't a dress you can trade in for a trendier version! It's the only one you've got.

In the United States today, the girls and women who fit the beauty standard tend to be . . .

- much taller and slimmer than the average girl. Only about 5 percent of women actually have the body type of a typical model.

- nondisabled and cisgender. When did you last see a magazine model who uses a cane or a movie star who uses they/them pronouns?

- White. It's no secret that racism shapes who appears in TV, films, and advertisements. Less than half of kids in the United States are White, but you'd never guess that from picking up a book or turning on the TV! When women of color do appear in the media, they tend to have features similar to White people, like straight hair and light skin. That's just not right!

Beauty standards control people by telling them what to buy, how to dress, and what to worry about. But real happiness comes from *doing* good, not looking good.

picture-perfect or phony-boloney?

Girls learn about beauty standards from the images they see in the media every day. But those images are often more fantasy than fact.

Misleading magazines

Here's a behind-the-scenes look at the work that goes into making a magazine model look "perfect":

1. Image creators start by looking for tall and slim models who have facial features such as big eyes and a slender nose.

2. Professional stylists work their magic. They apply the model's makeup to look flawless. They add extensions to her hair to make it longer and fuller. They adjust clothing to look like it fits perfectly. If you ever see a model from the back, you'd see that her clothes are probably clipped and pinned!

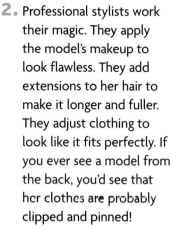

3. Photographers use fancy lighting and cameras to make a model look "perfect." They take hundreds of photos and choose just one or two that they like best.

4. After the photo shoot, artists alter the photos on a computer. They shape tummies, hips, arms, and thighs to look narrower—often narrower than physically possible. They smooth out the skin and remove lines, wrinkles, and stretch marks. They even lighten the skin tone, especially for models of color.

By the end of the process, even the models can have a hard time recognizing themselves! If you see an image that looks too perfect to be real, it probably is.

Suspicious selfies

Nowadays, anyone with a smartphone can do her own magazine-style photo shoot at home. With filters and photo-editing apps, girls can transform their face shape, smooth their skin, add wild colors to their hair, and even transform themselves into hot dogs! But studies show that unless a photo is using an obvious filter, most girls have a hard time noticing when a social media image has been altered. And even when girls *can* tell, an unrealistic image can still make them feel bad about their own bodies.

Playing with photos can be a lot of fun. But editing a photo simply to fit a beauty standard can hurt other girls. To play it safe, stick to the fun filters, like flower crowns, cat ears, and dancing bananas.

Dark side the beauty standard

Beauty standards may be made up, but their consequences are very, very real. They hurt girls by convincing them that their bodies are wrong. This stress can lead to:

Depression and anxiety

Dieting

Skipping meals and fasting

Smoking cigarettes

Vomiting on purpose or taking laxatives

Developing an eating disorder

Beauty standards affect even very young girls. More than half of girls ages six to eight wish they had thinner bodies.

If you live in the United States, it can be hard to imagine a world without the constant beauty pressures that come from television, movies, magazines, and social media. But one famous study from Fiji gives a glimpse into what that world might look like.

FIJI ISLANDS

SAVU-SAVU

NADI

SUVA

Fiji is a country in the Pacific Ocean where most people didn't have access to television until 1995. Traditionally, people in Fiji valued bodies that were robust and strong. Having a big body showed that you were a hard worker and had plenty of people who fed and cared for you. Eating disorders were unheard of. Then came television.

The shows that played on Fijian TVs came from countries like the United States, where thin was the beauty standard. Suddenly, girls saw bodies that looked a lot different than their own. They also saw advertisements for exercise equipment and diet products. After just three years, **74 percent** of Fijian girls said they were too fat. **Eleven percent** said they tried to lose weight by forcing themselves to throw up. In other words, TV created a beauty standard in Fiji that made girls sick.

DIET! LOSE WEIGHT FAST! Perfect skin! BLAST BODY FAT! BUY

It's tough to live in a world where beauty standards bombard you from every direction. But you do have some control over the images you see.

media makeover

If you watch television, spend time online, read magazines, or use social media, it's up to you (with help from your parents) to control what you see. Here's how to detox your media feed:

Step 1 — Pay attention.

If a picture or video suddenly makes you feel like you need to hop on a treadmill or buy goopy cream for your face—STOP. Something that gives you bad body feelings isn't worth your time.

Step 2 — Unfollow.

Make sure you stop seeing that kind of content in the future. Unfollow the account, change the channel, or unsubscribe from the magazine. (For the magazines you already have, use them for the art project on the next page!)

Unfollow

Step 3 — Change it up.

Look for kid-friendly content by Black, Latinx, Asian, and Native American creators. Find videos and images you like by people with big bodies, disabled bodies, and transgender bodies. Changing the bodies you see every day can change how you feel about beauty!

Step 4 — Keep it real.

As long as you've laid the ground rules with your parents, it's OK to post selfies. But when you do, show the real you. Show yourself doing things you love—like playing sports, cooking, or hanging out with your baby sister. No filters needed.

be-YOU-tiful

Put those old magazines to use! Grab paper and a pencil, and draw a picture of yourself (just an outline is fine). Then look through magazines for words and pictures that describe you. Cut them out. Also cut out shapes in the color of your clothes, skin, hair—plus whatever background you'd like. Use a glue stick to attach the clippings to the picture you drew. When you're finished, outline your features with a black marker. Be-YOU-tiful!

follow the money

If beauty standards are so dangerous, why do they persist?

One word: **money.**

Beauty standards stick around because advertisers want to make a profit. Ads tell girls not only that their bodies are wrong but that they can change their bodies by buying a product, trying a new diet, or exercising differently. The companies that make these ads don't actually care about health or happiness. In fact, they *want* you to feel unhealthy and unhappy so you'll buy what they're selling.

Here's a look at how much money beauty industries make each year:

$72 BILLION

- Americans spend $72 billion on weight-loss products, like diet shakes and weight-loss plans—even though 95 percent of diets don't work!

- Cosmetic products like eye shadow and razors bring in about $90 billion in the United States. About 85 percent of these sales comes from women. That means women have a lot less money to spend on other things!

$90 BILLION

$4 BILLION

- Americans who want darker skin spend $4 billion at tanning salons, even though tanning beds can cause skin cancer and eye damage. And across the world, people who want lighter skin spend about $8 billion on skin-lightening products, which can cause permanent scarring, thinning skin, and mercury poisoning.

$8 BILLION

When you're tempted by an ad, ask yourself: "How does this ad make me feel about my body?" If the answer is "bad," that product probably isn't worth your time.

bogus beauty bingo

How many of these common phrases can you find in the ads you see every day? Cross them off as you find them until you get five in a row. Then read more about each phrase on the following pages.

DROP POUNDS FAST	BLAST BELLY FAT	FLAT BELLY TEA	SHAKES	SUPPLEMENTS
JUST ONE CAPSULE A DAY . . .	WELLNESS	SUPERFOOD	NATURAL INGREDIENTS	FREE TRIAL
CLEANSE	DETOX	FREE	BEFORE AND AFTER	RESULTS NOT TYPICAL
SIDE EFFECTS MAY INCLUDE . . .	APPETITE SUPPRESSANT	SPONSORED BY	#AD	MY HONEST REVIEW
CLINICALLY PROVEN	DOCTOR RECOMMENDED	AND IT TASTES GREAT!	JUST FOR YOU!	ONLY A FEW LEFT!

DROP POUNDS FAST

Crash diets are the worst diets of all. Trying to lose weight fast can make you sick and harm your metabolism. In the long run, these diets lead to weight gain, not weight loss.

BLAST BELLY FAT

You don't have control over where your body stores fat. Doing exercises like sit-ups is great for strengthening your muscles—but it's not necessarily going to change the shape of your belly.

FLAT BELLY TEA

Any drink that promises a flat belly doesn't belong in your body. Many of these products simply make you poop faster! They can give you stomach cramps and diarrhea, and even make you poop your pants.

SHAKES, CAPSULES, AND SUPPLEMENTS

Is the advertiser your doctor? No? Then it has no idea what kind of extra nutrients your body might need—if any. Stick to eating a wide variety of foods, especially fruits, veggies, and grains.

WELLNESS

Diets sometimes sneak around under this disguise. Don't fall for it. A diet is still a diet, even if it has "wellness" in the name.

DETOX AND CLEANSE

Want to know the secret to cleansing toxins from your body? Having a liver and kidneys! These organs constantly filter bad stuff from your food and blood. A product that promises to detox or cleanse your body is a scam.

NATURAL INGREDIENTS AND SUPERFOODS

"Natural" doesn't mean a product is safe, healthy, or good for the environment. And "superfood" is just a way to say that a food has lots of nutrients, like most fruits and vegetables.

FREE TRIAL

You pay for "free" items, one way or another. A company might charge you for shipping, enroll you in a subscription program, or fill your in-box with ads. If an offer looks too good to be true, it probably is.

BEFORE AND AFTER

These pictures are easy to fake with lighting, poses, and, of course, photo editing. Don't fall for them!

APPETITE SUPPRESSANT

These products keep your body from telling your brain when you're hungry. That's bad news because listening to your body is *so important* for your health. Plus, appetite suppressants have long lists of side effects, like *insomnia* (not being able to sleep) and *constipation* (not being able to poop).

JUST FOR YOU!

Have you ever searched for something online, like how to get rid of pimples, only to see nothing but acne cream ads the rest of the day? Advertisers pay attention to what you do online and try to guess what kind of products you're likely to buy.

RESULTS NOT TYPICAL, SIDE EFFECTS MAY INCLUDE . . .

Look for these phrases in tiny, hard-to-read letters. Advertisers include them so people can't sue them when the products make them sick or don't work.

#AD, SPONSORED BY, MY HONEST REVIEW

These labels usually mean that someone is being paid to say nice things about a product. Sometimes they're true and sometimes they're not!

DOCTOR RECOMMENDED OR CLINICALLY PROVEN

Some businesses pay doctors to recommend a product, even if it doesn't work or causes bad side effects. And many companies do their own "clinical studies," which means they can tweak the results to make a product look good.

AND IT TASTES GREAT!

If an ad has to convince you that a product tastes better than it looks, it probably doesn't. Real meals are better.

ONLY A FEW LEFT!

Stores use this phrase to get you to buy products quickly, even if there's a whole warehouse full of them. Always research a product before you buy it. **79**

CELEBRATE

All bodies are
good bodies.
That's something
to celebrate!

81

put a stop to body talk

Talking about people's bodies can cause a lot of pain—even when you think you're giving a compliment! It's never OK to talk about other people's bodies. Period.

Here are some common body comments and how they can hurt:

YOUR WORDS	 your secret message	REALITY CHECK
"You're not fat, you're pretty!"	Only people in thin bodies can be pretty.	Bodies of all sizes can be pretty, including big bodies. It's easy to forget that fact when we see only thin bodies in the media.
"Wow, you're so tiny!" or "Holy cow, you're so tall!"	Your body stands out.	The person is probably tired of hearing this.
"I don't even notice your disability!"	The more you can hide your disability, the better.	Disabled bodies are gorgeous exactly as they are. They don't need to be fixed or covered up or made to look "normal" in order to be accepted, worthy, or celebrated.
"You look great! Have you lost weight?"	Your body didn't look great before because it was bigger. If it goes back to how it looked before, you won't look great anymore.	You don't know this person's story. She might be skipping meals, using dangerous weight-loss techniques, or even struggling with an eating disorder. A comment like this could encourage her to continue those unhealthy behaviors.

The best thing to say about another person's body is . . .

NOTHING!

If you have a thought about someone's body, keep it to yourself. Don't share it with the person. Don't blurt out your thoughts about the person's body after the person has left. Find something else to talk about and move on with the conversation.

My best friend thinks she's fat, even though she's just a bit chubby. I can tell she's very uncomfortable. We're in fourth grade, and a kid in our class keeps calling her fat. Every time I try to make her feel better about her insecurities, I chicken out. I'm afraid if I bring it up, she'll think that I think she's fat. How do I do it?

Hope, Louisiana

You're right that bringing it up would probably make her feel bad! Look for ways to help without commenting on your friend's body. First, stand up for her when she faces bullying. You could say, "It's never right to comment on someone's body. Please stop." If the bully doesn't stop, go to the teacher. Next, remind your friend of all the wonderful things you love about her. "You are such a good listener," or "No one can dance like you!" can help boost her confidence. Finally, stop talking about body sizes altogether, including yours. There are so many more useful and interesting things to discuss!

health myths

Sometimes body comments come disguised as well-meaning pieces of health advice. For example, you might hear someone say, "I think Alana would be healthier if she lost weight." Or, "All bodies deserve respect, but we shouldn't glorify obesity."

Attitudes like these don't help anyone have a healthier body. In fact, studies show that they result in *worse* health. Negative body comments lead to depression, lower self-esteem, exercising less, and disordered eating. The stress of teasing and discrimination is what's unhealthy, not having a large body. In fact, someone saying, "You probably shouldn't eat that ice cream sundae" could be worse for your health than the ice cream sundae is!

Still, people believe plenty of myths about what a healthy body looks like. Which of these have you heard before?

Overweight people don't live as long as thin people.

Nope! Research shows that people in the "overweight" category live as long—or longer—than thin people.

Being thin means you're in shape.

Wrong. People in big bodies can be physically fit, and thin people can be out of shape. Exercising regularly helps keep you healthy, no matter your body size.

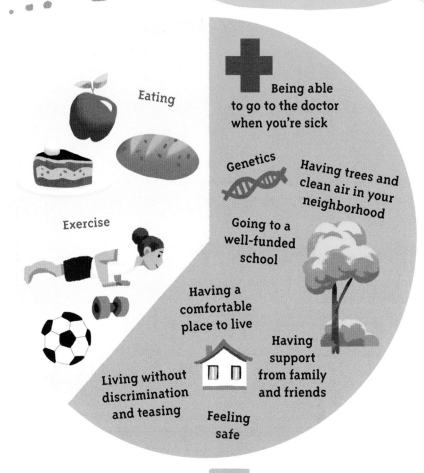

If people would just eat well and exercise, they'd be healthy.

Not true. Food and exercise account for only about a third of your overall health. The rest comes from factors out of your control!

Eating

Being able to go to the doctor when you're sick

Genetics

Having trees and clean air in your neighborhood

Going to a well-funded school

Exercise

Having a comfortable place to live

Having support from family and friends

Living without discrimination and teasing

Feeling safe

Things you control

Other factors

If you're tempted to make a comment about someone's eating or exercise habits, consider these actions instead:

- Volunteer at a food pantry to help families in your town get reliable meals.

- Write a letter to the city council about how more parks and bike lanes could help people get more exercise.

- Speak up when you see someone facing discrimination about their body.

food pantry

body bullying

It's a hard truth that some people have a tough time moving through the world because of how people view their bodies.

Just as *racism* means treating someone poorly because of their race, *ableism* means treating nondisabled people better than disabled people. *Sizeism* (also called *fatphobia*) means treating thin people better than people with large bodies. And *transphobia* means treating cisgender people better than transgender people. One person can experience multiple isms and phobias at the same time. They're all fancy words for a simple concept: *body bullying*.

Body bullying happens when people treat some bodies as if they're better than others. Sometimes it's obvious, like a person laughing at someone's disability or using a hurtful name. Other times it's sneaky, such as a school dress code prohibiting traditionally Black hairstyles like braids and dreadlocks or a restaurant not having a wheelchair ramp. Body bullying tells a person, "Your body is wrong. It should be more like mine!" It hurts, and it's wrong.

When you see it or experience it:

- Call it out for what it is, if it feels safe to do so. Explain that what's happening is wrong. You might say, "I'm proud of who I am, thank you very much," or, "This is hurtful. Here's why."

- Report it to someone who can help, like a teacher, counselor, principal, or parent. If the issue is big, you could even reach out to a local civil rights organization.

- Spread the news. Sometimes people have trouble spotting body bullying for what it is. To educate people, you could do a class presentation about how to make schools more accessible or create posters about using people's correct pronouns.

What other ideas do you have?

No amount of body love can cure body bullying

The reality is that no matter how much you love your body, how many affirmations you read in front of the mirror, and how proud you are to be you, you can still face challenges because of your body. That's not fair, and it hurts. But remember this: Your body is right. It's the bullying that's wrong. End of story.

making space for everyone

A world built on beauty standards tells people, "Sorry, but there's only room for a few of you at the table. Everyone else needs to go home." But a world that celebrates all bodies says, "Squeeze in, people! Let's make room for everyone!" A good example of how we've already made more room is . . . in the bathroom!

Toilet transformations

Think about the last time you used a public restroom. Was it easy to find one you felt comfortable using? Could you use it easily? Did you feel safe? How would your day have changed if using the bathroom meant going all the way home?

When public restrooms first became common in the 1800s, only men could use them. Being a woman meant that going out in public for more than a few hours was difficult. (How long can *you* go without using the bathroom?) But when women started working, participating in government, and entering the same spaces as men did, they demanded bathrooms. And they got them!

RIGHTS FOR WOMEN

HOW LONG MUST WE WAIT?

Not *all* women could use them, though. During the civil rights movement, Black women fought for the right to use the same clean, well-maintained bathrooms that White women used. They changed things by finally convincing Congress to pass the Civil Rights Act in 1964. Still, many women with disabilities couldn't use public bathrooms because most didn't have accessible stalls. These women helped Congress pass the Americans with Disabilities Act in 1990. Today, many transgender and nonbinary people are fighting for their right to use restrooms where they feel comfortable. Slowly but surely, they're changing bathrooms to be safe and stress-free places.

ALL-GENDER RESTROOM

Public restrooms make it possible for people to get jobs, go to school, travel, and do things outside the house. But to earn that right, did people change their bodies? Nope. They changed the *world*.

Imagining a different world

What changes would you like to see in the world? How can we make room for *all* types of bodies at the table? It's going to take a lot of creativity—and a bigger, more accessible table!

vision board

You will need:

- A piece of cardboard, as big as you'd like

- A piece of pretty fabric, a few inches longer and wider than the cardboard

- Craft glue

- Newspaper to cover your work space

- Thumbtacks

Directions:

1. With your work space covered, lay down the piece of cardboard. Cover one side in craft glue.

2. Carefully lay the fabric on top, right side up. Smooth out any wrinkles and let dry.

3. Turn the cardboard over and fold down the edges of the fabric. Glue the edges down and let dry.

4. Use thumbtacks to cover your vision board with photos, drawings, and images that make you think about a world that celebrates all bodies.

Real Girl RUNWAY

Jordan R. believes a little glitter can change the world!

Jordan has a limb difference, which means that her left arm didn't grow completely before she was born. For Jordan, that's not a bad thing. In fact, she decided to celebrate her difference by inventing a *prosthetic*, or artificial, arm that shoots glitter!

She spent months working on the design. The first version involved lots of glue and rubber bands. The final version is a purple, 3D-printed arm shaped like a unicorn horn. It uses an air compressor to shoot glitter from the tip when she presses a button. Jordan's device is so cool that the Museum of Science and Industry in Chicago put it on display!

"The Glitter Blaster has helped make people feel more comfortable around my limb difference," Jordan says. "Instead of staring at me, people stop and talk and laugh. Sparkles have a way of making people smile."

Now Jordan's helping other kids celebrate their bodies. She and her mom started an organization called Born Just Right, which puts on workshops for kids with limb differences. Kids can come up with ideas and work with experts to create one-of-a-kind devices that celebrate their differences, not hide them.

"Differences can be sparkly and awesome!" —Jordan

changing the world every day

Think of all the time you've ever spent worrying about what to wear, scrutinizing yourself in the mirror, or wishing your body was a little bit different. What else could you do with that time and energy? Here are some ideas!

Change your school

- Start a body love club.

- Do a presentation about racism in beauty standards.

- Write to the principal about your ideas for making after-school activities more accessible.

- Start a petition to make the dress code fair for everyone.

- Call out body bullying when you see it.

- Cover the bathroom mirrors in affirmations.

- Make sure school fund-raisers support people of all body sizes. For example, if your school sells T-shirts, make sure they come in big sizes, not just small sizes.

- Compliment people on their personality, not what they look like.

- Don't comment on people's bodies.

- Ask your social studies teacher for more information about the lives of people of color, people with disabilities, and transgender people during the time period you're studying.

- Join or create a group to unite transgender, nonbinary, and cisgender students.

Change your community

- Participate in a march that supports healthy body image.

- If you notice that condiments and napkins are out of reach for someone in a wheelchair, ask the restaurant manager to permanently move them to a better location.

- Ask people for their pronouns and use them correctly.

- Talk to the owner of a local business about putting up more inclusive bathroom signs.

- Create art featuring all kinds of bodies. Enter it in an art show.

- Ask a local theater to show a documentary about body positivity.

ALL-GENDER RESTROOM

- Join or start a book club, and suggest reading a book by a Black, disabled, or transgender author.

- Talk to a local librarian about creating a display of body-positive books.

BODY-POSITIVE BOOKS

Change the world

- Write a letter to a magazine or company that disappointed you. Explain how it could better support all kinds of bodies in the future.

- Report misleading and dangerous "health" ads. Show others how to do the same.

- If you post photos of yourself on social media (with parents' permission, of course), avoid misleading filters and editing.

- Call your elected officials and ask what they're doing to help prevent eating disorders.

- Research how certain people are silenced or discriminated against because of their bodies. Share your thoughts with others.

Your body is good. All bodies are good.
By celebrating all bodies,
we can make a world that's good.

resources

With a parent's permission, check out these resources to keep learning and to get extra help when you need it.

To learn more about or get help with . . .	Visit . . .
Gender identity	The Trevor Project (thetrevor-project.org) or Human Rights Campaign (hrc.org/resources)
Gender-inclusive schools	GLSEN (glsen.org)
Eating disorders	National Eating Disorders Association (www.national-eatingdisorders.org)
Bullying	StopBullying.gov
Diverse books	We Need Diverse Books (diversebooks.org)
Navigating a school or business with a disability	Americans with Disabilities Act (ADA.gov) or Disability Rights Advocates (dralegal.org)
Anti-racism	*A Smart Girl's Guide: Race & Inclusion*

Do you have a body image tale to tell?

Write to us!
Body Image Editor
American Girl
8400 Fairway Place
Middleton, WI 53562

Here are some other American Girl books you might like:

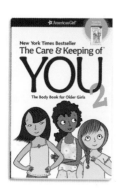

Each sold separately. Find more books online at americangirl.com.

Parents, request a FREE catalog at **americangirl.com/catalog**.
Sign up at **americangirl.com/email** to receive the latest news and exclusive offers.